LISTEN, TULLY!

Available in the Tales of Tully series

Tully's Life
This heart-warming story follows the journey of Tully from street dog to much-loved family pet, teaching young readers about the importance of kindness, understanding and hope.

Tully Takes Off!
Tully has arrived in her new home with her new grown-up, but she does not like it one bit! When Tully sees an opportunity to go back to her old life on the streets - the only life she has known up to now - she takes it with both paws. With a search underway, it is up to her new grown-up to work out what Tully needs and help get her safely home.

Tully and the Sad Day
Tully has woken up feeling grey and cloudy inside and she does not know what to do. She cannot help her big feeling because she does not know what it is. As her different feelings begin to work together in the wrong way, it is up to Tully's grown-up to help her to understand what she needs.

Go To Sleep Tully!
It is night time and Tully is tired, but she does not want to go to sleep. Her new grown-up knows that Tully is trying every trick she can to avoid going go to bed! With lots of adventures planned and Tully needing her rest, Tully's grown-up needs to find a way to help Tully learn to not be so worried about bedtime.

Tully and the Midnight Feast
Tully is a newly-adopted dog settling in with her new grown-up. Since her arrival, her snacks have started mysteriously disappearing from the cupboard and appearing under her bed, she seems to have forgotten her manners, and there are days when she just cannot stop eating! Tully and her grown-up need to work together to help Tully with her worries about food.

Tully and the Scary Day
Tully has woken up feeling scared. She isn't really sure why, but today feels like a very scary day, and she just wants to hide. Tully's grown-up is thankfully there to help Tully manage her big feelings and see that the day is not so scary after all.

Don't Touch Tully!
Tully is settling in with her new grown-up. She has learned that the new grown-up is a safe person and she enjoys strokes and cuddles with them. Then Tully starts to meet new people, who want to show her how loved she is. Unfortunately, Tully doesn't feel the same about people she does not know and trust. It is up to Tully's grown-up to find a way to help Tully with her big feelings and to be Tully's voice, when she can't use hers.

Tully and the Tummy Ache
Tully has a tummy ache and it's making her feel quite grumpy. She doesn't want to eat or drink, and she can't get comfortable. Her tummy is sore and it's getting worse! Tully is in a toilet muddle. So, Tully and her grown-up work together to sort the muddle out and help Tully to cure her tummy ache.

Tully's Birthday
It's Tully's birthday, and her grown-up has planned a special day for her, but Tully doesn't feel like celebrating. As the day begins to unfold, so do Tully's big feelings. Tully doesn't know what to do about the big feelings, so she does a bad thing. Luckily, Tully's grown-up is there to help her feel better about herself, and enjoy the rest of her birthday.

Listen, Tully!
Tully does not always like to listen, especially when her grown-up is trying to stop her having fun. Tully decides that instead of listening, she can be in charge. But when things start to go wrong, Tully and her grown-up need to work out how Tully can begin to find listening a little bit easier.

Tully and the Makeover
Tully has been having lots of fun playing in the mud, but now her grown-up says she has to have a bath. Oh dear! Tully is not sure she wants one of those. She is feeling a bit nervous about what is going to happen to her, but Tully's grown-up shows her that there is nothing to worry about. Having a bath is a good thing after all.

Tully and Vera
Tully has moved in with her new grown-up but she is missing her foster carer, Vera. Tully is struggling to understand why she had to leave, and whether it is okay to have big feelings about Vera. It is up to Tully's grown-up to try and help her to understand loss and endings and why, sometimes, they have to happen to make space for new beginnings.

Tully and the Chase
Tully loves to be chased. It gives her a feeling of excitement which starts off as being fun, but one day the excited feeling suddenly and very quickly becomes a feeling which is too big. Instead of feeling excited, Tully starts to feel scared. Tully and her grown-up need to work out how they can play Tully's exciting game without it becoming a bit too much for her, and causing a muddle.

Tully at Christmas
Things are starting to feel a bit different in Tully's house and all around outside. Tully's grown-up looks different, strange lights are appearing everywhere and people have started putting their gardens indoors! Tully is not sure what to make of this thing called Christmas – she just wants everything to stay the same. What can Tully's grown-up do to make Christmas-time a nicer time for both of them?

Tully Goes on Holiday
Tully has gone on a holiday with her grown-up. After a difficult start, things seem to be going well. But when the fairground opens up, with all its flashing lights, loud music and food smells, Tully's big feelings get the better of her, making her want to run. And she does! Tully's grown-up needs to find her in time to show her that holidays can be fun after all.

Tully and the New Rules
Tully likes lots of things about living in a house with her grown-up, but one thing she really doesn't like is all the rules! Tully thinks the rules are all very boring and her grown-up must want to stop her from having fun. One day Tully breaks her least favourite rule, and something bad happens. Tully doesn't know what to do! Can Tully's grown-up get to the bottom of this muddle so it doesn't happen again?

Listen, Tully!

TALES OF TULLY

Jess van der Hoech

Trauma Tools
& Training

Acknowledgements

As always, to my trusted editor Sarah Ogden for all that you do to make these books come to life. I will never fully know what goes on behind the scenes, but it is a joy to work alongside you on these projects. Thank you.

Thank you to my supervisor Linda Hoggan for your continued support, encouragement, discussion and much-welcomed feedback on this series. I learn so much from you and the knowledge I have gained form our conversations has been invaluable across my practice, the books and now this series. Thank you.

Thank you to Laura Benham, for your support in giving me feedback, the searching questions, your friendship and of course, the countless conversations about dogs, the content of which has become quite useful! Thank you.

To the children and families who I meet in my therapy room, from whom I have learned more about hope and healing than any course could ever teach me. Your input, ideas, questions and answers are so valuable to me and I will be forever grateful. Thank you.

Preface

The *Tales of Tully* series is based on the adoption of an ex street dog from Bosnia who came to live with me in September 2023. Watching her try to settle and adapt from everything she had previously known to fit in with a new way of life began to present a number of ideas as to how to communicate such difficulties that can be experienced, to others who are in the process of adopting or who have adopted children. The aim of the series is to provide an opportunity to explore different situations, circumstances, feelings and experiences, finding new ways of communicating and understanding each other, through the voice of Tully.

When Tully first came to me from Bosnia, she would not look at me, never mind listen to anything I said! She was so fearful and it took a long time for her to begin to trust me and to know that I can keep her safe. As the trust between us began to develop, she started to learn that I was the keeper of the treats and by following instructions, good things would come!

Interestingly, Tully still won't take even the highest reward treats from my son who lives with me. She will eat a treat that he has left next to her when he has left the room, but she will never let him see her eat it. These treats are sniffed and inspected for a prolonged period before she will eat them, but if I was to come and pick up the exact same treat and give it to her, she would take it immediately. Tully has learned that as I am the one who does the work with her, I am her safe person and she can trust me.

This does not mean that she always listens to me of course, particularly when she is enjoying a late night zoomie around the garden! We are still working on her recall but I am confident this will come with time. The more we practice, the better chance she has of learning what it is that she needs to do.

Tully and I both needed to adjust to be able to bond in the way we have. I needed to re-establish my expectations of her, because her early life experience as a street dog taught her a lot of lessons that she needs to unlearn. I needed to become completely predictable to her – we needed to learn about each other.

The same principles can be applied to children who are struggling to listen. This could be at home, with friends or family members or at school. First and foremost, a child needs to know that they can trust the adult who is giving them instructions. It is not unusual for children to want to be the boss when the world around them does not feel as safe as it possibly could be; this includes needing to know who their safe grown-ups are.

If a relationship built on trust is established first, the child is more likely to listen to that person and follow instructions. Sadly, not all grown-ups have always been safe in every child's world and so the theory that children should listen to all adults all of the time is not always easily implemented.

Through the story of Tully, the child and grown-up can begin to have conversations around the importance of safety, trust and the skill of good listening.

How to use this book

First and foremost, ensure that both you and the child are well-regulated and comfortable when you begin to read Tully's story. Make sure you choose a time when you are unlikely to be interrupted. The child may like a soother, a favourite or fidget toy, a drink or something to suck or chew to help them to stay regulated.

If the child is calm, then begins to try and distract or move away from the reading, make a note of what they have just heard in the text. It is very likely that they will have just provided you with some valuable information about something that they cannot tolerate or want to avoid for now.

The questions have been designed not only to explore the internal world of the child, but to help to develop a common language between the child and adult who are using this book together. The child cannot get the answers to the questions incorrect. Their interpretation of the thoughts and feelings Tully is having may provide some very significant information about the child's own thoughts and feelings. The child may want to expand the answers to talk about themselves and may even be able to make comparisons between Tully's feelings and their own.

Listen, Tully!

Tully was playing with her ball in the garden. It was really good fun and she was having a great time.

"It's time to come in now Tully!" she heard her grown-up call. Tully didn't want to go in. So she didn't.

Tully heard her grown-up call again. She used all her concentration on the ball she was playing with so she did not hear her grown-up anymore.

Why might Tully be doing this?

Tully saw her grown-up come into the garden. Tully got a big feeling. The grown-up walked up to her and clipped her lead onto her collar.

"It's time to come inside now Tully," the grown-up said, and led her back into the house.

Tully felt very cross. The grown-up was always spoiling Tully's fun. It had been much better when Tully was little and she was a street dog in Bosnia. There were no grown-ups to tell Tully what to do. She had got really good at looking after herself then, so why couldn't she do that now?

How might Tully feel about having a grown-up telling her what to do?

Tully didn't need anyone. She could be the boss. Tully decided that she would not listen to her grown-up anymore.

Is this a good plan?

Later that day, Tully – who loved zoomies – decided she would do a few in the kitchen. Tully was not supposed to do zoomies in the house. But she was in charge now. So she did. Running in circles, spinning really fast – Tully loved it.

"No zoomies in the house Tully," her grown-up said. Tully didn't listen.

The grown-up told her once, twice, three times and suddenly, Bang! Tully crashed into the kitchen cupboard, hitting her head. Ouch!

How is Tully feeling now?

Could Tully have done something differently?

At snack time, Tully's grown-up prepared some cheese for her. Tully loved cheese. The grown-up gave her four small cubes of cheese. It was delicious.

"No more, Tully" the grown-up said, even though Tully was looking at the rest of the cheese with her best pleading eyes. Tully's grown-up did not want her to have any treats!

When the grown-up left the room, Tully jumped up onto the counter and got the rest of the cheese. She was in charge now and she decided that she would finish the cheese.

What made Tully take the cheese?

Why does Tully think the grown-up said 'no more?"

"Tully! I said no more cheese!" the grown-up said, seeing the empty cheese packet on the floor. Tully didn't care. She had enjoyed that cheese. It had taken her mind off of her sore head where she had hit it on the cupboard. It was still hurting. Now her tummy was starting to ache from all of the cheese she had just eaten.

Tully needed to get back outside to play with her ball. She scratched at the door.

"Later, Tully," the grown-up said.

"Why later?" Tully thought. "I want to go out now while the hot sun is out." Tully was not happy with her grown-up. It was a good job she was in charge now.

How is Tully feeling about being in charge now?

When the grown-up went outside to put some rubbish in the bin, Tully sneaked out too. She ran around the garden, onto the path, across the patio and away from her grown-up who was now coming to get her again.

"Inside, Tully," the grown-up said. But Tully was in charge so she stayed where she was.

After a few minutes, Tully began to notice a feeling in her paws. The sun had heated up the patio and path and it was making Tully's paws very sore. Ouch!

Tully's grown-up noticed Tully had stayed still and so went to pick her up to bring her back into the house where it was cool.

How is Tully feeling?

How is the grown-up feeling about what Tully is doing?

Tully's grown-up looked at Tully who was feeling a bit sorry for herself. Her head hurt from the bump, her tummy ached from the cheese and her paws were sore from the hot patio.

Tully's grown-up put a cooling mat on the floor to help Tully's sore paws, fetched her a drink to help her tummy and sat and stroked her sore head. Tully noticed that her grown-up was still caring for her, even though she had not listened to them all day.

"I know that you are still learning that I am keeping you safe, Tully," the grown-up told her. "I know that you used to look after yourself when you were little and did not have to listen to anyone.

"I ask you to listen to me because I am keeping you safe. I know that zoomies are not a good idea in the house because there is not enough space. I told you to come in because the sun was getting too hot, and I didn't let you eat all of the cheese because I knew it would make your tummy hurt. I tell you to listen to me, because I am caring for you."

How does Tully feel about this?

Does Tully like having a grown-up to care for her?

Sometimes Tully's grown-up did seem like they were spoiling her fun, but Tully knew that she was in her safe house with a grown-up who loved her and was keeping her safe.

Tully and her grown-up agreed that the grown-up would be the boss of the house and Tully would be the boss of her body.

Maybe she could start listening after all.

Listen, Tully!

About the author

Jess van der Hoech is a qualified therapist who has spent the last ten years studying and working with the impact of developmental trauma and, in particular, the assessment and treatment of children and adolescents with complex trauma and dissociation.

As well as supporting birth families, Jess works with looked-after and adopted children and families, using skills in attachment-focused therapy and therapeutic parenting techniques.

Jess is a supervisor, trainer and motivational speaker with a passion for writing therapeutic books that are accessible to children and families to help with the healing process and to increase awareness in the impact of trauma.

Also by Jess van der Hoech

What A Muddle (2016) ISBN 978 18381987 0 1 (Co-authored with Renée Potgieter Marks)
An interactive, practical workbook designed to help children who have difficulties with emotional regulation to begin to understand what is happening in their bodies. A variety of activities throughout the book enable the child to start to explore these ideas through the story of Sam, while gently encouraging them to begin to verbalise their own experiences. Carrying out the physical exercises in the book can promote changes in emotional regulation. The text is written in a child-friendly, gender-neutral style, and is easy to understand for parents, carers and practitioners alike. For children aged 4-12.

These Three Words (2018) ISBN 978 18381987 5 6
Also available as an e-book. A unique therapeutic novel for teenagers with the aim of linking together the feelings, emotions and behaviours connected to anxiety, with some of the therapeutic tools that can be used in order to enable better self-regulation, increased confidence and different ways of thinking. The book is equally valuable to parents of teenagers with anxiety, giving them an insight and understanding into some of the issues that may be affecting their child, and potentially opening up a line of communication and a way forward between parent and teen.

These Three Words: The Journal (2019) ISBN 978 18381987 2 5
A thought-provoking and hands-on workbook, combining a series of practical exercises and tools designed to assist teenagers who are struggling with the symptoms of anxiety. Addressing the anxious responses in both brain and body, this journal provides the reader with the opportunity to discover therapeutic coping techniques and learn how to apply them to their own personal problem areas, before committing to a twenty-eight-day practice to promote good emotional regulation and reduced anxiety. The journal can be used alongside the therapeutic novel These Three Words, or as a standalone workbook, and it is suitable for use by the teenage reader on their own, with a parent, or in a group.

Beastie, Baby and the Brand-New Mummy (2022) ISBN 978 18381987 3 2 and *Beastie, Baby and the Brand-New Daddy (2022) ISBN 978 18381987 4 9*
A therapeutic story that looks at the external signs of pathological dissociation in a child. Dolly's story helps children who have experienced early trauma to begin to understand, in a very simple way, what dissociation is and why it has happened in their internal world. Tools and techniques are included within the story that parents and caregivers can use to assist the child in the first stages of their healing process. Beautiful illustrations on every page enhance the story of Dolly, and help the reader to relate to the events that happen, to notice the methods Dolly has developed to manage her feelings, and to think about what is happening in their own internal world. For children aged 4-12

Printed in Great Britain
by Amazon